Miracle of Days

Anthony Mills

Miracle of Days

Acknowledgements

'Assent' and 'The End of the Road' were published previously in *Burrow*.

Miracle of Days
ISBN 978 1 76109 442 2
Copyright © text Anthony Mills 2022
Cover image: Anthony Mills

First published 2022 by
GINNINDERRA PRESS
PO Box 3461 Port Adelaide 5015
www.ginninderrapress.com.au

Contents

Part 1: Bitten by Love: Poems on the life of Francis of Assisi

   Knight Errant   11
   Pietro Bernardone   12
   The Leper   13
   The Wolf of Gubbio   14
   Brother Ass   15
   Brother Leo   16
   Canticle   17
   Francis among the Crusaders   18
   The Courtesan   19
   The Cutting of Clara's Hair   20
   Lady Pica   21
   Nightwatch   22
   The Word   23
   Stigmata   24

Part 2: Exiles

   Ferry Crossing   27
   Adam's Issue   28
   The Equilibrist   29
   Breathing Underground   30
   Ecce Homo   31
   The Man With the Golden Helmet   33
   Assent   34

Part 3: Grief Lessons

   Legacy   37
   Snow in the Highlands   39
   Farm Shed   40
   Silvery Moon   41
   The Crying   42

Jasmine	43
The woodcutter	44
Taboo	46
Coat	47
Death of a Father	48
Tallowwood	49
Leaving	50

Part 4: The Longing World

Childhood	53
These are the days I love	55
Town	56
Kite	58
The Treehouse	59
The Night My Brother Nearly Choked to Death	60
Bicycle	62
Rainlight	64
The Children's Cemetery	66
The Meat Market	67
Tapping	68
The Beat of the Early Years	70
Watching My Hands Grow Old	72
Wintered (Hordern Street)	73
Orchard Thieves	74
Elemental	75
The Square, Early Morning	76

Part 5: Loopholes

Miracle of Days	79
Day Into Night	80
Firescape	81
Coastal	82
Mount Carnarvon Lookout	83

Harbour	84
Praying Mantis	85
Storm Fabric	86
End of the Road	87
Winter Morning, Bundanoon	88
Life Saving	89
A Wedding	91
Planting Oranges	92

For Jenny

Part 1

Bitten by Love: Poems on the life of Francis of Assisi

For my Mother and Father

Knight Errant

His beardless face in bloom,
wearing painted armour and colourful cloak,
Francis carries a feathered lance of olive wood,
the god of his desire lays the road before him.

The trembling of horses swims the air,
draws his scarfed mount striding to a band of
young fellow warriors, they swerve
towards a towered town swaying in the heat.

In the tear-stained streets, in the sour air of
rattling carts stiff with breathless bodies,
birds throat-silent carry bitterness in their beaks,
the bells of sorrow raw with sounding.

He wonders to what he has entrusted his faith.
His heart grows dark, soul tainted with fruitless
prophecy, the wound living within torn open
runs large like floodwater.

Pietro Bernardone*

When I ask him for his obedience
to follow me and the hoard I have built,
he returns the clothes from his back, naked
in front of all disclaims me father, to inherit the wind.

My heart broken by anger, face a runnel of tears,
bones twisted by his infidelity.
What gulling God demands
the life of my first-born?

Francis dismisses me, a slave straiten by grief.
I shiver into the night, cold as a thousand stars,
the darkness a shroud for my shame.

My son, what froward fancies you follow:
you betray your filiation for
the fabled treasure house of the heavens.

* Francis's father

The Leper

Conceived in an eclipse and born
in yellow days cold with stone,
devil-struck by the black wind
ballasted at times by only his bones.

Restless with a bellowing itch,
shame clamours the crawling amputee,
toes and fingers beaten-unmade
a portion for dogs, gobbets black as tea.

The lean-jawed Francis timid and slow
crackles from a quake,
sheltered in his voice a swollen
music incarnates.

The saint kisses the festered body:
released from the captive walls of blight
sweetness burns 'cross the leper's skin,
leaping from the dark's rib, light.

The Wolf of Gubbio

In gratitude he welcomes the night.
Howling with age,
hungry enough to eat the earth,
the grass curving as he skirts the town of sleepless mothers.

Troubled by morning he keeps to the forest.
The trees gnawing the light,
the cold clatter of his soul,
hate making him lean.

Then the Saint with stretched arms,
a handful of calm, a word of grace.
His wolf heart bows down as he gulps
the offered silence,

weeds clear from his mind.
Brother sun traces the trees silver,
birds tell the world how
sister moon sprouts in his heart.

The town fragrant with smoke,
the fields turn to subtle flower.
The wolf becomes Gubbio
Gubbio becomes the wolf.

Brother Ass*

The roads thick with temptation
this poor penitent powerless to oppose,
trampled by a savage heart
I have numbered all your bones.†

Scarred hide and blood-blotted
sorrowing and sullen you babble,
the laughing mob grabbles you on your knees,
your griefs countless as the covetous rabble.

Standing your shrieking shadow upright,
grinding your teeth on winter,
the moon of affliction rises in your skull
your bray the sleepless stars splinter.

Brother Ass I have wronged you,
I have beaten you with a love askew.

* Brother Ass is the name Francis gave to his body.
† The line 'I have numbered all your bones' is from Psalm 22.

Brother Leo*

From his journal

Sowing his all-night tears on my cheeks,
my body shaken, head full of knots,
Francis smells of the wind and endless snow,
eyes all soul in the purple darkness.

His raw voice a tangle of light
flares from his desire for the greatest thing.
Promised paradise is too distant,
on living earth, we mirror perfect love,

where wonder and madness are mistaken one for the other.
From the peace and quiet of poverty
he breaks into flower, his happiness unbound.

Day rises from his shuddering heart,
heads lifted to heaven, our song astonishes the air,
we sing like throated sparrows rising from the grass.

---

* Brother Leo was a constant companion of Francis.

Canticle

These blessings come flaming, blaze and startle me.
A wing sound clear as a lute
ignites my marrow to exalt the new-feathered day.
Captured by the shivering trees, the violet oatfields,

the chestnuts blooming white, pearls of dew
dripping dreams, every stone, all have a voice.
My eyes washed by rain, skin stained and wind-wrung,
my clay ears tuned to the harmony of emptiness,

a quavering concord, gladness glows in my heart.
Then song babbles in my every cell,
I, Francis, songster to sun and moon,

troubadour of earth's rhythmic music
know her soft benediction enfolding all,
what day does not know the sound of its soul?

Francis among the Crusaders

On the shores of evening Ancona
his weather-cock mind scans the sky for a fortunate sign,
chanting prayers measured by his heart's beat,
voice ebbing on a darkening tide.

Disembarking on the Sultan's shores
the clangour-jangle frenzied-strife,
armies trample the fields with widow-swords
ballast the world with bones.

A twitchy wind filled with whispering dead
buoys Francis to the Sultan's tent,
grumbling like camels the sentries usher him in.
The ruler of the faithful, ringed fingers flashing,

silk slippers glittering, aches with laughter
at the sight of dishevelled Francis.
Raucous in their imitation, caged vermillion birds
imprisoned by their brightness.

Face now silent, leaden in the last light
he offers Francis a drink and signals for him to speak.
Tickling his tongue with spice, Francis exclaims
the fragrant wonders of his God.

The sultan's numbed mind sinks in the raven-fed fields,
his words freeze then thaw:
'reft of rhythm our only music is death
we have shut our eyes and cannot find our way back.'

The Courtesan

When I clutch his hands
he shakes like a snared dove,
voice quiet as prayer,
jet dark eyes a spark among straw.

Used to the perjuries of men
tongued in my throat,
this shaggy-headed god intoxicate
untrained in the art, fires my bones.

I impregnate the air with promise:
a plump-bellied night
ploughed round a feathered furrow.

Spineless worm he runs,
mouth a savage loathing bellowing *punk*,
his head full of deserts, his heart's forest withered.

The Cutting of Clara's Hair

Barefoot, dressed in clay
he spreads a sacred ash circle,
words sing from him like
swallows threading ribbons through the sky.

His warm breath touches my face,
his gaze closes my eyes,
my hair gathered in his hands.
In the soft movement of scissors I am shed.

My body too narrow, the world too small,
I cry like a bird in first flight
the air upholding me.

My soul sails among cloud banks,
my unravelling I offer to mute eternity,
I am nothing and everything.

Lady Pica*

No mystical inbreathing conceived you, my son.
I was forced to couple and bore the brunt,
my belly stripped by your birth.

Clothed with my flesh, the grace of my womb,
I warmed you in the night, touched you with kisses,
remember the milk from my breast?
You like a calf gambolling – a sour-sweet time.

Your heart now emptied of me,
given to another for the asking.
In pain I bore you, in pain I let you go.

I stuff my bed with stone, shave my head.
Cradling joy, prayers flutter between my lips.
My heart nestles in obedience,
swaddled in the suckle-brown of poverty.

---

* Lady Pica was Francis's mother who, on the death of her husband, became a nun.

Nightwatch

From Brother Leo's journal

On the beating wings of night,
in sleep the dreams come.
A myriad of voices, the bristling howl
of wolf-dark shadows, the shrill supplication of lepers.

His blind-feet mind laying out the roads,
flailing at murderous shapes, the panting breath,
the madness in marrow, the wound
living in his poor heretic heart.

In the huddled shape of destitution, he wakes.
Tears follow the indelible furrows of his face,
body drained dry. At the mouth of his cave
the saffron dawn touches heaven, suddenly

he grows taller with the seeds of fire, his voice
now strong as steel, wrapping the earth
in an excess of song that buttresses the crumbling world.

The Word

And the word was made flesh: John 1:14

Fixed to the earth, fashioned in claggy clay
my heart brabbles like a pauper's weary ass.
Your word struggles among the urban roar
of each day's sorrows and brittle joys.

The brightness dark with your telling, you spoke
not from any cloud but from a sound –
the ragged moan of a leper, a tattered rag,
a handful of hair-bone bound.

In this body I bear my sins
pressed through every vein and skin,
I have purged this flesh of its flesh
loved this flesh for its flesh,

I feel the fullness of its days falling.
In its revelation the word is love.

Stigmata

From the diary of Francis, Mount La Verna, 1225

Dawn burning, its fierce colour soundless,
my cracked face turned to the intense light.
Beaten by night I limp forward, feet tangled,
my tongue tied with your name.

You found me among the rocks and woods,
saved from the teeth of wolves
with no weapon but the word.
My frail frame stretched, ribs fallen,

blood thudding, I extend my arms in joy.
Bitten by love I bleed.
Gazing at my oozing wounds, my body broken
my hope scourged; I desire nothing.

Close as breath is hollow-eyed death, outside
grumbling to God, the ass waits to carry my body.

Part 2

Exiles

Ferry Crossing

Aeneas frees Misenus

Men mill on the riverbank like bees, anxious
for the ferry. The air shivers the molten river,
trapped shadows uncurl as night slowly shreds.
Quibbling quail bury in the long grass, the stones
wake from sleep, stutter under restless feet.

Scribbled on trembling water a tail of light from
a clatter-clank fishing boat fleeing black night.
Drowsing nets, dishevelled and empty, hard-question
the man on deck. The boxed helmsman, straight-backed,
strains at the wheel, the river rippling kicks the bow tearing her.

The day gains sound, its troubled music laps the ear:
bitter cries shake from the air above as gulls
battle the boat; the sky drags rain-laden clouds
rumbling at the horizon; twisted tea-trees
broken-necked, head-bang the shore.

Bent by heavy thought, temples splintered, I stare
into the haunted river, unwinding with remorse,
sound the breathless pain of his drowning death.
I try to fix his face before me, my vision sand banked.
Bound by the river, I offer prayers for his release.

Then I see him spring from the dark water
like a flying fish wheeling through spacious air,
the wind wound round him, a shade that escapes
my embrace. When I sight him at the crossing, he turns,
waves as he jumps silently onboard the ferry.

Adam's Issue

Cursed be the soil…thorn and thistle shall it sprout for you. – Genesis 3:17

During those first blue days
the perfumed flesh of naked earth
smelling of birth,
the air gentle as bird breath,
his mind warm with the soil.

Here and there a patch of silence,
crows preening in the red gum,
the short lives of shadows retreating
as earth became sun drunk.
A man unashamed of his innocence.

Now, in these thistle days,
a plough worked from the tree of his knowing
lies smashed like bloodied sorrow.
Brother that envied brother.
The muttering of thorns entangling the earth,

the last of the flock sand-blind,
his hair wild with tearing.
Mind incessant with the voice
condemning him to dust and
the breath leaving him.

The Equilibrist

Balanced atop a swaying wire
the high priest of a dangerous religion.
Below, the dazzled congregation,
mouths stretched like windsocks,
their tongues tremble against a fall.

Like a dancing spark he moves
against a landscape of running shadows,
breath balanced against breath.
The coursing spotlight pursues him,
his lean body bitten by the light.

Then silence as at prayer,
at the moment of sacrifice.
Standing erect, arms outstretched,
a cry hovers on his lips,
face torn with the effort.

A communion of held breaths escapes.
A murmur of voices, then Hurrah! Hurrah!
Yells lance the air as he somersaults
with a jubilant lightness to earth,
sated heart sprung open.

Breathing Underground

The old man's cough rattles black
weighing the dust-filled wind,
his cinched breath grapples at unreachable words.

Straiten on his enamelled lawn,
rushing clouds dodge
the litany of names sprinting

from the greyhound track across the road,
the rot in his lungs his pit inheritance.
When the ambulance arrives

they raise him, solemn as a lean prophet,
into the stark white van.
I sit, the dew descending, watch

his dog chase them down the street
dragging the marrowless sky,
the weight of a life breathing underground.

Ecce Homo

When they brought him out
                            I was in the crowd
loaded with my weekly shop at the market.
                                I heard the din
from the government buildings
a shrapnel of words
                        the crowd rabbling for his life.

News reports later said he was a pathetic
                        comic figure
                              the weight of a child.
All-gash, Shiraz-dark blood spreading like ink
                                        from his head
his face bloated, fear crawling along his bones.

Someone had thrown a purple cloth over him
he stumbled against the wind
       fell a few times
              as he was grappled to a waiting van.
The crowd
              whose heart formed no prayer
were mouthing like demons
                        hoarse in their wilding
for the release of a footballer
       guilty of rape.

I noticed at the back
       those jugglers of empty words egging the crowd
              pounding the nail of hate.

  I wash my hands of
    these public humiliations. Often they are
      Outsiders
  on their marrow for a place of refuge.

The sky was getting dark
  it looked like we were in for a hell of a storm
  I decided
    to leg it
      for   home.

The Man With the Golden Helmet

From the Rembrandt School, 1650

In the prism of the moment, the uncertain light
pries at the secrets of his half-eclipsed face.
Indelible veins river the loose flesh,
emaciated cheeks sallow with grief, shadows anoint
his forehead, axe-knocked with knotted thought.

His helmet-strapped ears contain the weary chatter,
a myriad of confused voices huddles in his brain.
His unwinking eyes lost in a passing gallery of memory,
the retrospect dead dragging the years of war,
disturbing reason, hope scattered like smoke.

His bent-over heart crowded by a cry,
anger kicking against the wall of his body.
Kallo* etched in his brain, retreating men drowning
in the swelling river, pawing the air in the morning's darkness,
their cries for help strangled by artillery fire.

Grey light edging over the rim of the earth, bloated
bodies laid out along the shoreline, their eyes,
like jewelled grapes, ripe for picking by massing gulls.
A prayer for each man hovers on his lips, a handful of sand sifted
as a last rite, until he kneels, exhausted, unable to move.

Now painted by eternal shadows threatening the light,
brushed by the eloquent lie of hero, the colour of defeat
fills his lips, face a landscape winnowed of vigour.
His mind forever walks the shingle banks of the river,
swerving with sorrow, and calling the names of the dead.

* The battle of Kallo, one of the bloodiest battles of the Eighty Years War.

Assent

'I'll bear affliction till it do cry out itself "enough, enough", and die.'
– Gloucester, *King Lear* 4.5.

The grey light of early morning bent over earth
splinters on tidal pools retreating under rock.
Huge sets of curling waves land with the green
weight of sea-shudder, trampling the bay.

Gulls flash like steel, sharpen their shrill voice
against howling wind; knotted strings of kelp
litter the beach; a fishing boat flounders among
clashing wind and light.

Atop cliffs imagined, a man plucked blind,
wind-wrung, wrestles grief. Hostage of chaos,
his mind's knives prod him to the cliff's edge.
Far below, the sea struggles with its undercurrents.

Flinging himself into air, he falls not far and soft,
dead in his imagining. A pulse of breath blows
inwards, his death startles to life.
Humbly feathered he yields to a new sky,

his mind cloudless, free from fear,
heart buoyed in the blue air of assent.

Part 3

Grief Lessons

Legacy

'a second grief this harsh will never touch my heart' – Achilles, *Iliad*

Each morning my mother's young sister
helped make breakfast,
the Early Kooka at chin height.
Stirred the oat porridge
till it became thick and shiny,
set the table with plate and spoon,
with joy and laughter.

At each place she stopped to name its sitter,
her clear voice like a herald
calling them into being.
They appeared in pyjamas,
thick sleep still in their eyes,
the winter cold pushing into bare
feet skating the linoleum floor.

She the youngest, godlike,
until a trampling black breath
lodged in her blood.
She felt her weakness, the cold secret
and then suddenly, like a god, was gone.

In the dark twilight, the leaves
on the oak tree wasted and died,
scourged by the rough hand of the wind.
In their grief, the family shouted like cranes,
their cries rocking the walls.

When the priest came, his voice
buried in his chest,
his tobacco-stained fingers anointed
her eyes, nostrils, and star-like mouth.
Then, with no sins to be forgiven,
he left to trudge the night road.

On the day they laid her down,
her lungs loaded with the full weight of the earth,
the grass rippling deaf to tears,
what song could sing her back?

My mother's voice broken,
her face battered by sorrow,
she collapsed like a tower in the dust.
Her heart now weighed by a heavy stone
that only silence could carry.

Snow in the Highlands

My father's shadow
wire-bent
on the ice-spiked earth.
His thin papered hands
barbed, raw and bleeding
as he strained against
the last fence post.

Just past noon
he lay spreadeagled,
trying to fix a breath
that wouldn't come.

From the west snow-clouds
string-lined the hills,
the valley stretched
white and wounded,
voiceless,
under the snow.

Farm Shed

In the lambent dawn
dust drifts to a fusty corner.
In the spent shadows
aback stacked drums,
a thieves-clinch of rusted
roof-hanging enginery,
stolen earth dangling from their tines.

A morning seventy-five years ago.
The earth falters under a burning light,
the wind out from its storehouse.
My grand-father dry as hay,
already raw with the work of his day,
struggles with the cutter
bellowing its yellow noise.

Like a bloody ambush it rears,
the machine rams him
like someone detested,
mingling his bones with the stones.
The sheep in the next paddock
stand bewildered and frightened,
under a broken tree.

My grandfather rises slowly,
a staggering mound of earth.
The wind marking him,
hounds him to the shed.
As if he could see the future
in the dust falling from him,
he creeps into the shadows and never returns.

Silvery Moon

on the drowning of a two-year-old girl

Through the door
she sees the child
again and again,
sitting on the back veranda,
her face, hair, eyes, smile,
singing the moon song,
while they draw with chalk.

Guiding her arm
across the frail sky,
the clouds traced with her name.
A flash of light enclosed in her face
with the promise of a falling star.
Twilight of sandpipers and boobook.

Everywhere the signs:
swelling pillars of cloud,
the migrating rattle of mullet,
jangle-alarm of birds,
a half-built sandcastle falling
at the edge of the changing tide.

Now she sits drawing
a child's name
again, and again
in the shifting sand,
singing to herself,
watching waves
return to water.

The Crying

A distant dog
howling
accompanies the slow sobbing
of the child in the room downstairs.

The dog's lonely heart,
its dark emptiness
echoes across the valley,
settling like fog
above the sodden ground.

A ground so full of tears
that it cries
underneath the footsteps of a child,
a ground so sad
it makes a child weep.

Jasmine

The day my grandmother fell,
tangled in her stroke, crushing bodies
of purple hyacinths, she lay half-
swallowed by a freshly dug garden trench.

Her breaths scudded among puffball
dandelions ready to journey,
her last, snatched flowering jasmine
squeezing a toppling wood-shed.

My grandfather bent in the curve
of his sunny chair, crying out,
knew that this was wanton
death shifting from the shadows.

Months later he flayed the garden,
tearing its skin in large pieces,
leaving her wishing tree untouched.
For months he woke to the illusory

sounds of breakfast clatter and radio hype,
kissed the lips of cold air. Haunted by the blue
stare of each day, became thinner and mute,
mouth a hard knot around her name.

Summer evenings he sat by her tree,
cicadas scoring the last breaths of day,
falling light splintering the yard,
the scent of jasmine peeling his mind.

The woodcutter

As a child his father had him chop wood
behind the family general store,
the mulberry sky pressing on its roof.

A slow blindness from the creeping twilight,
air trembling amid the barked trees
in the near paddock, its heart eaten by drought.

He stopped to rag-wrap his raw hands,
spat the wonted blisters
from the rough-hewn axe handle.

The wind's decaying breath
filled his throat, his tongue dust,
his hairless face lean as rock.

Stacked the yellow-honeyed wood (to be sold by the cord)
against the growing darkness.
As he washed in the outside laundry

a hesitant star climbed the emptied trees.
At night he woke from dreams filled with ghost-
trees keening on the bones of the wind,

the stiff land desolate of shade,
a soundless sky of blenched light.
In the uneasy dawn he felt as rootless as a wisp of smoke,

felt he was drifting above the ground.
The one day spent in the wooden school,
red dust wandering the face of the windows,

the swift sky singing in his head,
he turned his hands over
pressing his calluses with pride,

an unfeeling hardness that grew from the rusted earth itself.
In later years it was the pain of pain remembered,
the rag of memory, that undid him.

Holding his head with scarred hands to steady himself,
silenced by the dumbness of truth,
the heartache of a man unblessed of childhood.

Taboo

My grandfather's heavy woollen coat,
brass helmet, fireman's boots, and axe,
once votive and argus-eyed
now accusing him.

One night he was called to the edge of town,
to a fire so great it wounded the air.
A huge prayer-house of flame
that pushed itself to the clouds.

Much later he returned home,
haggard as a hunted bird.
His raven hands, a dumb show, split the air
assailing an impenetrable door.

There was nothing he could explain.
His mouth struggled like a landed fish,
he shook cold as dark water,
a jinn had struck him senseless.

A man fetid
with burnt flesh,
the breath in his nostrils ever reeking.

Coat

After you had died,
picked from the pile
destined for the charity shop,
a welcomed fit,
it whispered escaped time –
years woven upon years.

From the shadow of your old age
we leaned into winter sun.
Skin eroded, hands like maps,
face crazed, voice story-shine,
coat – raising memory to light.

On its sleeves the shuddering forest,
sky breaking in where trees toppled.
Wheedle of whistle and whip-crack,
bullocks laboured under logs,
tearing muscle up swelling hills.

The long fingers of dusk,
glass-winged dragonflies
trickling over creek flats,
emerged from pocket flaps.

Firelight dogs, flat and breathless,
heavy with dust.
Crackle of voices sparking
from dark swags, blue night
stitched with loose scent of rain.

A long silence and I would look
to see you distilled to light,
dozing in bright sun.

Death of a Father

His sickness an unseen plague thrusting
nothing in front of her but his bewildered
body stamped into its white sheet,
a ragged noise from his fallen mouth.

A daughter ensnared, trapped by his broken breath,
her tangled words finger his face in the darkening room.
Unable to forbid the rhythmic whispers of fear,
her mouth swallows prayer at the hard work of dying,

her body twisted with the grey knot of grief.
A doctor offers her a stethoscope,
a kindness helping unpick her taut weave of sorrow.
She hears the doubletalk of her heartbeat and her father's,

his falling, a receding echo, hers pounding
like a girl locked out, begging to come inside.
Finally, stillness, as if a door had been opened
on a sky wide with stars.

Tallowwood

At the edge of the forest
pulling at its heart, a whirling tree.
Branches criss-cross in the shadows,
panicked lifelines snatching at
petrol-perfumed air.

In the warm end-light of an autumn day
the tree uproars, wavers senselessly
falls
bouncing,
a final shudder.

From the near paddock
black ducks scatter, losing their direction.
A pained plover harries the sun down,
a double drummer rising from earth-sleep,
hardening into shape, battles the empty air.

A novice light grieves the forest floor,
chainsaws tremor in the thin shade.
The downdraft slow, a cortege of noiseless leaves,
a twirling alphabet of the dead,
grazes on dust.

And I
turn to track a cold caw, a black dart
thriving on loss, tossing earth
among exhumed roots, bending
beak-sharp at his forensic examination.

Leaving

The tears of leaving are hidden
in the soft drone of our voices.
You prepare to quit your accustomed
spaces, spurning the claimed dazzle
of light, the ascent into a windless sky.

Little by little, in the morphine-laden air,
you lean towards those beckoning shades
at your bedroom door. Outside, hysterical
parrots entangled in a shifting wind, veer
back and forth screeching for release.

Muffled in sheets, body bent in a curve,
spasms of pain crushing you, the remaining
life in your body dark, impenetrable.
Behind shut eyes, you overturn mind's stones
for lost loves, wading deeper into yourself.

The flesh of morning taut with truth –
your mouth open asking nothing.
Through the open bedroom window
a pulse of wind shivers the room,
the day shrinks, hardens into an unfamiliar face.

Part 4

The Longing World

Childhood

Then I loved
the smell
of blood-warm
bread
from the horse cart

the lowing
of the factory
whistle,
the smoky air of
joking men
nudging
parrot biscuit tins
in the half light
corner shop.

The unknown woman's
handkerchief spittle
on small, grazed knees,
broken shells on the footpath
the earth smell of
egg yolk.

The kite,
its wild escape to
the tall gum,
string-burnt hands.

The tall cypress
beckoning,
wasp hiding,
stings
that hurriedly brought bluebag
from the laundry.

Grace
for lamb and three veg

Father
singing,
the very model of a modern
major general.

These are the days I love

Autumn days,
the red flash of a bullfinch
in the mock orange
a frozen blue sky.

Washed white sheets gently kiss,
line-drying in the garden breeze.
Budgerigars non-stop chatter,
far off a rooster crows.

The stabled horse hails
the clapping of pacers
on the bitumen road
heading for the track.

The sun in my bones,
basil and the heavy purple
of eggplants, ribbon sweet corn
and white bean flowers.

The gentle sea breeze
skating our rooftop and
you in the garden chair.

Town

Still
the morning
wet winter's light.

The houses on the plain
before the forest hills,
silvereyes in the pear trees
magpies nestling in the pines.

Black dust on the rooftops.

At dusk
the mine whistle
herds home.
In each hearth
a coal fire,
smudged faces taste
smoke-stained air.

Beyond the church steeple
the green sea,
ships wait, empty.
The seamed headland
butts storm clouds,
fishermen cast nets at
the rising moon.

Twilight, insistent mothers
call from bull-nosed verandas
their voices echo
against the escarpment.

On the beach
children leave behind
moulded soft sand,
the ruins of shell life.

Kite

Dowel, brown paper, string
on the backdoor step.
The dowel cross a rib
to spread the taut paper skin.

Tail of stockings and ties,
in summer used to hold up
sagging tomatoes.
When I first flew my kite

it smashed againstatree.
Wind took the string
from my hands, burnt
them as it tugged.

Those string-scars like a grass-
hopper in clasped hands,
prised open at school
on the street

so that doubters could run
their fingers along the rough
healing skin to confirm a rumour
or win a bet.

The Treehouse

From the top branches
entangled among sails of cloud,
I could look out over the whole
lacklustre suburb toward

a hazy, incomprehensible future.
I lived behind a dream, a wall
against the dictatorship of repetition,
and dark noise of the world.

A soft-boned tendril, I climbed far,
breaking through sky to enter
silence and secret,
the world turning soluble below –

houses crouched under shadow,
TVs blue webbing windows,
the acrid sweat of traffic staining air,
light snaking in pools.

I climbed down each evening to dinner
among flatlanders. Weighted
by exile, stuttering over my day,
I endured the burden of the grounded.

Later, the tree, struck by lightning,
shattered across our yard.
Sentenced to ground, lost to sky,
I spent days sawing firewood.

The Night My Brother Nearly Choked to Death

Late dark of summer day
cowering under drumming rain,
night shapes skirting streetlight,
cars – their heat and slur lagging
wet-back streets, filing into driveways,
tethered in their iridescent slick.

Two by two, we six children bathed,
set aside in dressing gown and pyjamas.
My mother, in the sway of sifting
and salting, conjures dinner. My father
in his chair, mauled from work.
TV settled in its corner – Bob
and Dolly Dyer corralling us, *'customers'*
on British Petroleum's *Pick-A-Box*.

A sudden commotion from the bathroom,
my father, panic veining his eyes,
dangles my three-year-old brother by the legs
over the bath, thumping his back,
my brother choking on a small floor tile.

Braids of memory – Mother herds
us out the house, her prayers whispered
out loud, my father balancing his son's
life under one arm, all of us huddled
into the neighbour's front porch
where my brother threw up the tile.

He stood beaming at us, sky-faced,
entranced at this sudden attention,
his body an unsettled gravity, as if lifting
to another country where voices soft
and coaxing glimmered in the dark.

For a short time, we joined him,
an inrush of light lilting us
then shrugged off, ground-fallen.
Later, some old fear entered, like a thief
touched with the scent of night, leaving
its skulking shadow hovering in our blood.

Bicycle

Most winter mornings
we dressed in the cold
beside a coal fire
that did little to warm
the flat room we ate in.
Tendrils of light crept
through venetian blinds,
Willow cups and bowls,
oranges, half-lit on a silky-
oak dining table.
Family meals silenced
by unspoken hurt.

Outside the sun stalled
on unending sky, trees
swayed to a vast chord
of bitter south wind.
My new blue birthday
bicycle, ribbon-frosted.

Each week, from butcher
to home, a carefully
balanced quarter of beef,
separated into back
and front panniers –
weekends swaying
on brown roads, filled
with tight cylinders
of newspapers, flung
into dusty yards.

One afternoon, racing
from class to bike shed
I found it gone.
Tired of the weight of
silent mornings,
the uneasy balance
along pockmarked streets,
it set out in the leafless world
trying to trace its purpose.

Rainlight

The shimmering city
beams from wet
sunlight's tumbled dive
across buckled steel and glass.

The green flare of summer
sways over burnished streets,
silky air curves among the swish-
drizzle of cars, thunder trembles

through towers of cloud.
Sharp shoulders of sky-
scrapers shape sunlight through
fine wires of rain, drawing
benediction to barefoot streets.
Parking cars shy the kerb,
splashing puddles, freeing
rainbows to splatter

shop windows. Water runs
down drains, an artesian river
gushing to the harbour
where gulls bob in trance

alongside tinkling yachts.
The Opera House, rain-
blurred sails white as linen,
is anchored by strains of stillness.

From the bow of a ferry
heading to the zoo,
my father, throwing off silence,
names each passing bay,

glistening arenas of blue.
I toss between his tender
intoning and snatches of
light riding waves.

The Children's Cemetery

On this hill looking over
where the abandoned town
wraps the river,
wind sown with breast-beaten voices,
morning light skips into
cracks in stone walls
a blessing upon grass and earth.

Angels toy as lookouts
on the watch-stone monuments.
Diphtheria, whooping cough, influenza
one day, two months, five years,
graven names gnawed by the rain,
scotch-hoppers from the wailsome houses below.

Across the river
the new town,
a rising tide
of squeals and yells
swinging from its banks
sweeps to the great ocean.

The Meat Market

The overpowering mixture
of flesh and sawdust.
Carcasses hanging on hooks,
chops and sausages,
legs of pork, sides of branded beef,
quiver in the windows.

White-coated men
from refrigerated vans
load and unload
the dead weight
under a septic
blue sky.

The smell of promised barbecues,
burnt faces and pot bellies,
belching fathers screaming mothers
and children
dangling
from trees.

Tapping

For weeks now the bird has been flying
around the house tapping at each window
in a furious way, tapping its code of dashes
and dots as if it had an urgent message to deliver,

a message that no-one is paying any attention to
except to try and frighten the bird away.
From dawn to dusk, resting only for a little while,
it keeps flying at the windows, tapping out its message.

What does it want with us? Is it lonely,
wanting companionship? Was it abandoned
at birth by parents who couldn't cope?
Is it a portent of good or bad luck?

When she came to us from the orphanage
at the age of four, my foster-sister would stand
looking out of her bedroom window gently tapping
on the glass as if testing the strength or fragility

of her new place or to survey a way of escape.
Like a bird she gathered our precious belongings,
built a nest with them in the middle of her bedroom floor.
Nestled in her world among these things,

she hoped she too would become precious,
that she would have a name to be known by.
We thought that she was taking what didn't belong to her.
Not knowing her language we labelled her *thief*.

Outside, the bird flies from window to window
keeps tapping, tapping into memory,
tapping in a language we know nothing of,
tapping how we fail to hear the need for love.

The Beat of the Early Years

We germinate in sleep
seed of spooling light
shuddered into pulsing day.

Mouths innocent of words,
hungry cries bone-white,
hard as future longing.

Faces veined with hope
eyes heavy with soul
ears tuned to clamour,

sharp voices roaring
across a table-land clatter
of life pitched poor.

School days stranded
scribble crackled against heat.
A rumple of black-robed nuns

swinging beads staccato-
tick-swept corridors with fear.
Weekends blue blaze striking

between rusted goal posts.
As adolescents we whittled
down into boredom, disbelieving

the story of our lives   the dry
rattle of days kicking up dust,
blood echoing the thudding

metre of factory bass
across the road.
Stars tracked us through

wasteland smelling of lust,
hearts crashed in dead grass
broken black and blue.

Watching My Hands Grow Old

Hard to believe that they were once
no larger than a dolls,
that the fingers delighted
in furling and unfurling,
the vice-like grip.

Once they held a cricket bat
in the washing line pitch,
passed handkerchief-knotted coins
to the first-school-day bus driver,
spent lazy afternoons searching for eggs in the fowl yard.

Later, grubbing new potatoes in the backyard,
strumming a light-blinding summer,
forever restless, yearning in
the picture-theatre dark,
fingering a new life's grip.

Now these hands are snakeskin thin,
rasp-rough, ragged.
Gnawed by the thief of days and
nameless loss running sand
through their scarred fingers.

Wintered (Hordern Street)

Winter, a reckless time.
Spinning winds against the land,
the torn sky dangling loose,
light-headed birds in leafless trees.

Night slows to a crawl,
falls through trees to rusted earth.
The years beat down on my head,
memories flutter, like the air between my hands.

Newtown 1973.
The coolness of delicatessens,
thick slices of corned beef and milk,
light soft as birdwing.

Hordern Street – a road that dreams take.
My feet on uneven ground,
a nineteen years-old weanling
confounded by the bright light of the world,

an acolyte in the dark folds of forfeit,
anxiety a muzzle on my mouth.
Possums gibbering on the roof
return me to now,

a man with a moon over his head.
I listen to the stars,
the sighing of the house,
watch the grey dawn spill into the sky.

Orchard Thieves

Like our first parents
we stole through gardens
to taste the pith of life,
the god speechless at our effrontery.

The world smelling of sleep,
our guilty eyes bruised
moon-washed fields,
the trees heavy in the hanging bright.

In the middle of the orchard,
recalling our ancestors,
birds alarmed the world like gongs,
stunning the air with their noise.

With tangled feet through devil's grass
we ran our desire naked
into the endless shadows,
our faces hidden; our paradise forsaken.

Elemental

Your ashes poured into cupped hands,
I am amazed – the small pebbles,
bits of metal.

Your fascination with fire started early,
the back fence caught one Saturday,
best of all, the vacant grassy block

starbright on Christmas Eve.
I hand you slowly to the waves,
knowing we all start like this

Earth and water drunk by the wind,
the same wind forged your life
hard as pebble-steel.

This morning, the day star fractures
the air – crystal waves, light dripping
from surfers returning to the shore.

The Square, Early Morning

The yawning light, just created, earth-bound,
flowers among nests of stone in the silent square.
The black and white prancing-chatter of magpies, wings
like tattered banners, hostage the cafe awning, their acidulous
eyes jerking, watch clouds curl in the glistening windows.

The wind's thin steps measure the ground, stir spent leaves
hunching in corners, their colour drying out in death.
Casuarina shadows spin splintered patterns on coloured tables
bolted to the ground; a pendant of dew drips from
stacked chairs, splatters the pavement.

A stale taste of last night's carousing, trodden under feet,
washes to the gutters, shepherded by a man sloshing
through the early light, slender fingers blue in hard grip,
a hose pulsing under its skin. A twitching shock of yellow light,
a truck cranes bins to its rotten belly, stumbles down the street

hissing in stop-start fury, squeals at a smiling dog in its path
wrestling bread from a torn brown bag.
Morning full-fledged, hops on sparrow-coloured cobbles,
covers, in growing richness, the centre of the square.
Light all-embracing, astonishes the longing world.

Part 5

Loopholes

Miracle of Days

Consider the sun-washed stones,
how they shimmer and cry in the afternoon blue.
How the crab crosses the land
in a never-straightforward manner
with pincers raised to the moon.

Watch her unbound grain-coloured hair,
as she splashes like a diving bird.
Fish sprinting below kiss her giddy feet
as she dawdles the sandy bottom,
dreaming like a whimsical goddess.

Think how a child taking a bird from the air
marvels at the softness of its body,
claps song across the morning fields,
her mouth opens to the sky
for the feathered rain.

Regard those who arise under the morning star,
how they pray to placate a howling storm
for those belied in narrow-bellied boats,
or feed a multitude with a handful of bread
to become sweet honey in their mouths.

These are the signs that crowd my days,
the coming out of ourselves,
banishing the false dreams that roost in our hearts.
Though our names mark meagre mounds
we are beyond beginning and end.

Day Into Night

The city settles into red twists of cloud
combing the remaining threads of daylight across
a long rib of stone that braces the harbour foreshore.

Waves of scented wind from across the water
stir among palm trees lacing the Botanic Gardens,
their fronds shiver in the encroaching darkness.

Across the vast body of the harbour's green sea
a fine mist of rain weaves among first stars stepping
out along the sandstone cliffs of Balls Head.

Whirring fruit bats sail out like serifs, sonic
pinging swerves them at last moment from collision,
their ink-black wings fold and unfold in the crowded air.

A ferry sways, intoxicated by salt, signals final crossing,
its name brushed on oily waves tapping timbered piers.
Last light slips and slides along hulls of eggshell-white

yachts that dangle in bays; the iron web of the bridge
filigreed by the disappearing sun. I first saw dark light
ribbon my young father in hospital, the year of his sickness.

I watched his shadow on the wall fold and unfold, grapple
each breath, grateful when he slept, a humming stillness,
the city emptying and the dusky light.

Firescape

From the roadside the black hills and valley,
naked bodies of trees on their knees,
their arms stretched among gutted wheat.

Paddocks calloused by hard labour
hide in plain sight
ash spattered sheep, strewn under the humming sun,

rags of skin shrivelling on their bones.
A dead horse, stiff among burnt out rails,
its hobbled legs shot in the air.

On the wind a bird cry vaporises in the heat.
A drumbeat pulses the air, hidden among scourged trees,
a 'roo, thumping the crackling skin of the earth.

The dead wheat quivers, the rhythm
pounds to your feet, running into your blood and ears.
Back riding in the car the road

flees like an animal in fright,
twisting and turning, wide-eyed,
black body snaking hunchbacked hills.

Coastal

The old path to the bay is broken by forgetfulness.
From the headland, a long descent to the beach,
not a soul to be seen, just black-winged birds
wavering above the dragging sea.

As I step down onto the steep remains of the track,
silver streams of cloud herded by the wind
rush by like a god's breath that leaves no trace.
A widowed westringia, sun-stricken, crouching

like a pile of bones, crumbles as I grab it.
I slip on rocks rounded by attrition,
dig my hands into the earth to hold steady,
my heart a flapping rag, pearly sweat blistering my face.

Reaching the beach, I wash my face in the swash,
breathe the salt-seasoned air.
Oblique-eyed gulls bicker like children on holiday,
their grievances sail the wind.

I rest against the dark-bodied cliff,
spilling waves gabbling over the scree.
The world drunk on its talk cuts me loose,
my name lost to the grace of things.

Mount Carnarvon Lookout

Climbing the hill, a bird-black chain
pulls me the last meters to the sky-scraping clouds.
Far below the speechless river tongues the valley,
cloud-shadows huddle the humped hills,
pied currawongs chant their vesper office.

Before me, where once the sea shouted over the land,
a huge god-smashed rock
carries the sky across its back.
The leaves of over-weathered trees hang in sighs,
their turquoise breath honey in my throat.

I stop to catch what the heart has gathered,
and all at once the sky's thin sphere
becomes a trapdoor for the mind.
A flowered silence falls
across the boundless evening.

Harbour

Small cove landlocked
except for the mouth,
refuge from the
black sea.

How I miss your warmth,
curve of your back,
the ridge of your
breakwater spine.

At night
my hand reaches
in a slow swim-stroke,
I dive,
full moonlight
across an empty
shore.

Praying Mantis

The morning fresh-cracked,
a yoke-yellow sun among
the sky's pale flutter.

Green as new leaf,
from the air assembled
a mantis raises its arms,

lean as hunger.
Drawing its leg over the earth
marks a favoured place.

Alert to the constellation
of flies above,
mind hot with lust.

Like a priest trading his god for idols
he strikes in an orgiastic fury,
hands juggling the kill.

Blended with the world,
a prince of pagans,
he settles to eat.

Storm Fabric

Needles of light, whiter than silence, weave onto earth.
Black-clothed clouds, sewn over dawn, threaten rain.
In a corner of bent sky, lightning rips warp and weft
of morning; the air curls, waves of thunder shudder.

Trees tangle, branches rippling, bow to obey the wind.
Sodden birds, fastened to trunks, ache from tearing rain,
their song losing thread. Leaves shuttle, wind-ferried,
crowd against yellow grass taking cover among rock.

A rush of water overlays bare soil, reveals
a hidden seam knotted with taut wad of roots.
A cord of crows, impatient at morning's dark wing,
claw tight on a weeping crab-apple's wild swing.

Sky-concealing clouds stitch-ripped, rain sun-gagged,
startled shadows pale from sudden brightness,
green light shawl-wraps a delicate shoulder of hills,
soft pouches of sky float in a breathless heart.

End of the Road

This winter seems colder.
You can see it in the way
trees shiver their last
leaves, the way the earth
lying heavily, hesitates to
touch them when they fall.

Everything is ice and dirty
white. Cloud-smoke skims
streets, smudges eyes,
vision constrained to middle
ground. Walkers amble paths,
rugged within their loneliness,

echoes of their feet beat
underground. Day circles
its end   wilting light running
black lanes, wind-scattered
shadows, spasms of sharp rain,
birds folded in feathered frames.

I walk to the end of the road
where the quarry begins
wondering how I grew old
so quickly. Ahead
a wallaby, light-shivered,
strums the ground with its paw,

bounces out of sight through
a loophole in the air,
leaving behind a sudden dark.

Winter Morning, Bundanoon

A raw morning, the sky soundless,
a weeping light metal grey.
Frost-gnawed empty-trees,
the bald ground muttering prayer.

I wake, round-eyed, the claw of night embedded,
skirting dream shadows-
an eyewink of the long boat of the dead
sailing winged light.

Stepping onto the back porch
my shadow casts me fixed, silence-wrapped.
Heart spiced with the salt of dawn, eyes lift to
The Lake of Dreams, dark in the setting moon.

As if they had taken flight,
the dead summon mist
to anoint stones, trees, and grass,
leaving the whole earth dangling in mid-air.

Life Saving

A day flattened by summer's hand,
the sky a vast bleached shell,
silver-dazzle waltzing the sea.
A crowd of querulous birds

scratch a warning on the wind.
Prodded by the thin fingers of desire
into the black, thick water,
I swim to where the waves braid,

threading their secret.
Stairs of sand slip beneath me,
entangled shadows huddle like gravestones,
the sea tramples my head.

I grasp for air like a shameless beggar,
the past enrobed, heavy with regret.
Set to hand my name back,
a nuggetty lifesaver, thin as a snapper

rows with wings, the wind whistling.
His hand of grace pulls me on board
as shearwaters snatch fish mid-flight,
the water speechless with envy.

Back on shore walking with light,
my breath counts its clayed steps.
The sweet dreams of insects thrum the air,
a glistening from the wild yellow Acacia

running the dunes behind the beach.
An heir to a rising salt-sated moon,
I am unweighed of my past,
requiring nothing any more.

A Wedding

Immersed in the union of morning light
and warm sea air, the church, albescent,
leans towards a marbled bay.
Along a rim of shoreline
knotted reflections of resting boats,
brief hopes of little waves.

Today among family and friends,
I stand around a pool, drink in hand,
feel the benevolence of my pulse
ticking in its case; overheard voices –
the price of houses, the names of new
great nieces and nephews.

Somehow, floating in like driftwood,
from death's ocean, my father's voice,
sounding among undulating talk,
prompts me to wish my niece
the ordinary day's wonder, and a heart
able to endure the world adrift.

Planting Oranges

The living blue of a winter morning,
down on our knees
planting orange trees in wimbled holes,
my nine-year-old hands clumsy with the cold.

Your laugh from across the row
when milky rain spattered your upturned face,
the arms of the earth holding you there fixed,
you who spat your spittle into my blood that made us brothers.

Looking far down the row, your sister appears
half buried in the earth like a goddess.
When we stop for a break,
splitting oranges with a knife

the flesh as dark as blood,
an eagle skirts the tops of the laden
trees in the next row,
a long whistle hovers in mid-air

stuns me to dumbness,
my ears suddenly dug open
to how we sing
the earth into being.

www.ingramcontent.com/pod-product-compliance
Lightning Source LLC
Chambersburg PA
CBHW070311120526
44590CB00017B/2622